*Allonby village (Stage 5)*

## WALKING THE KING CHARLES III ENGLAND COAST PATH: NORTH WEST – CUMBRIA

This guidebook describes the Cumbrian section of the 590km (367 mile) King Charles III England Coast Path in the north west. It covers the National Trail from Gretna to Grange-over-Sands along the Cumbrian coastline. This convenient and compact booklet shows the route, providing all the mapping you need to walk the trail in either direction.

### Contents and using this guide

This booklet of Ordnance Survey 1:25,000 Explorer® maps has been designed for convenient use on the trail and includes:
- a key to map pages (page 2) showing where to find the maps for each stage.
- the full and up-to-date line of the National Trail designed for use northbound or southbound.
- an extract from the OS Explorer map legend (pages 89–92).

The companion guidebook – *Walking the King Charles III England Coast Path: North West* – describes the full route in both directions with lots of other practical and historical information.

© Cicerone Press 2025
First edition 2025
ISBN: 978 1 78631 029 3
Photos © Ange Harker 2025
© Crown copyright and database rights 2025 OS AC0000810376
Printed in Singapore by KHL Printing on responsibly sourced paper.
Cicerone's EU representative for GPSR compliance is Easy Access System Europe, Mustamäe tee 50, 10621 Tallinn, Estonia. Email gpsr.requests@easproject.com.

## THE KING CHARLES III ENGLAND COAST PATH: NORTH WEST

| | | |
|---|---|---|
| Stage 1 | Gretna to Knockupworth | 6 |
| Stage 2 | Knockupworth to Bowness-on-Solway | 11 |
| Stage 3 | Bowness-on-Solway to Abbeytown | 14 |
| Stage 5 | Abbeytown to Silloth | 22 |
| Stage 6 | Silloth to Maryport | 26 |
| Stage 7 | Maryport to Whitehaven | 32 |
| Stage 8 | Whitehaven to Seascale | 40 |
| Stage 9 | Seascale to Ravenglass | 48 |
| Stage 10 | Bootle to Silecroft Beach | 53 |
| Stage 11 | Silecroft Beach to Green Road railway station | 57 |
| Stage 11 | Foxfield to North Scale | 62 |
| Stage 12 | North Scale to Vickerstown | 69 |
| Stage 13 | Vickerstown to Bardsea | 69 |
| Stage 14 | Bardsea to Cark | 76 |
| Stage 15 | Cark to Grange-over-Sands | 84 |

Stages 16–28 . . . . . . . . . . . . . . . . . . . . . . . . . . . Lancashire & Merseyside booklet

### Route symbols on OS map extracts

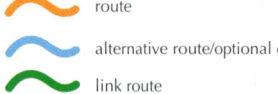

— route
— alternative route/optional detour
— link route

(SF) start/finish point
(SF) alternative start/finish point

for OS legend see printed OS maps

SCALE: 1:25,000

0 kilometres    0.5    1
0 miles              0.5

**GPX files**
for all routes can be downloaded free at
www.cicerone.co.uk/1029/GPX

*Crossing Grune Point to meet its western shore (Stage 4)*

*The wild cliffs of Annaside and Gutterby Banks geological SSSI (Stage 9)*

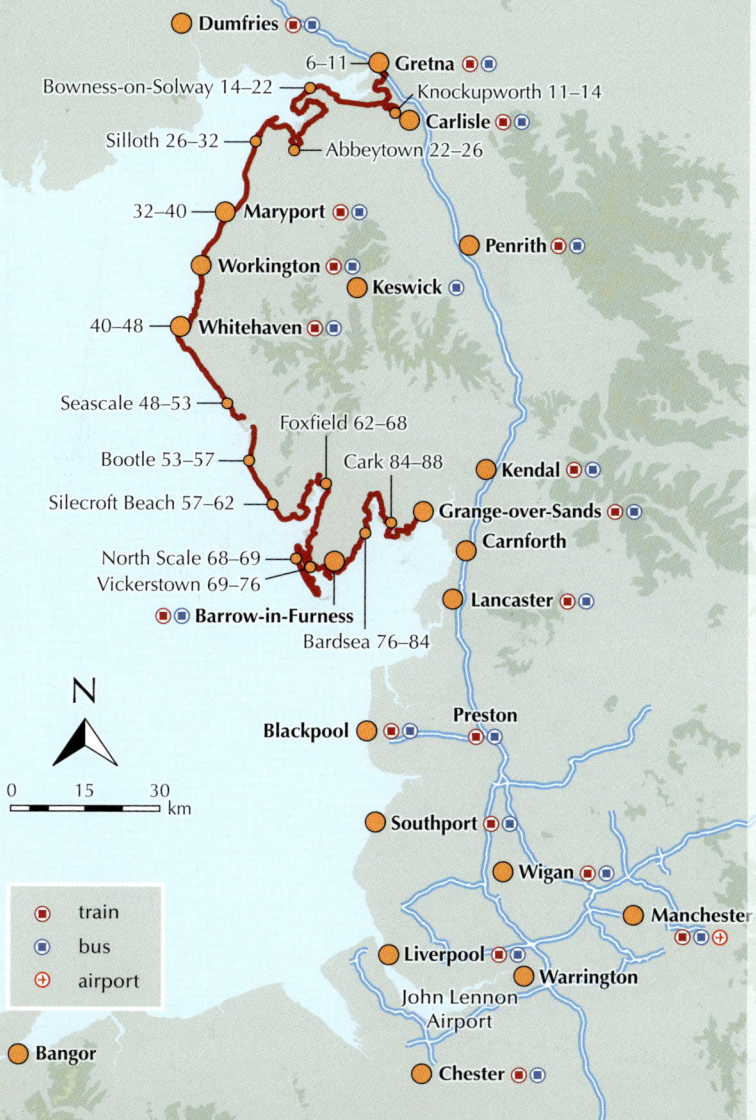

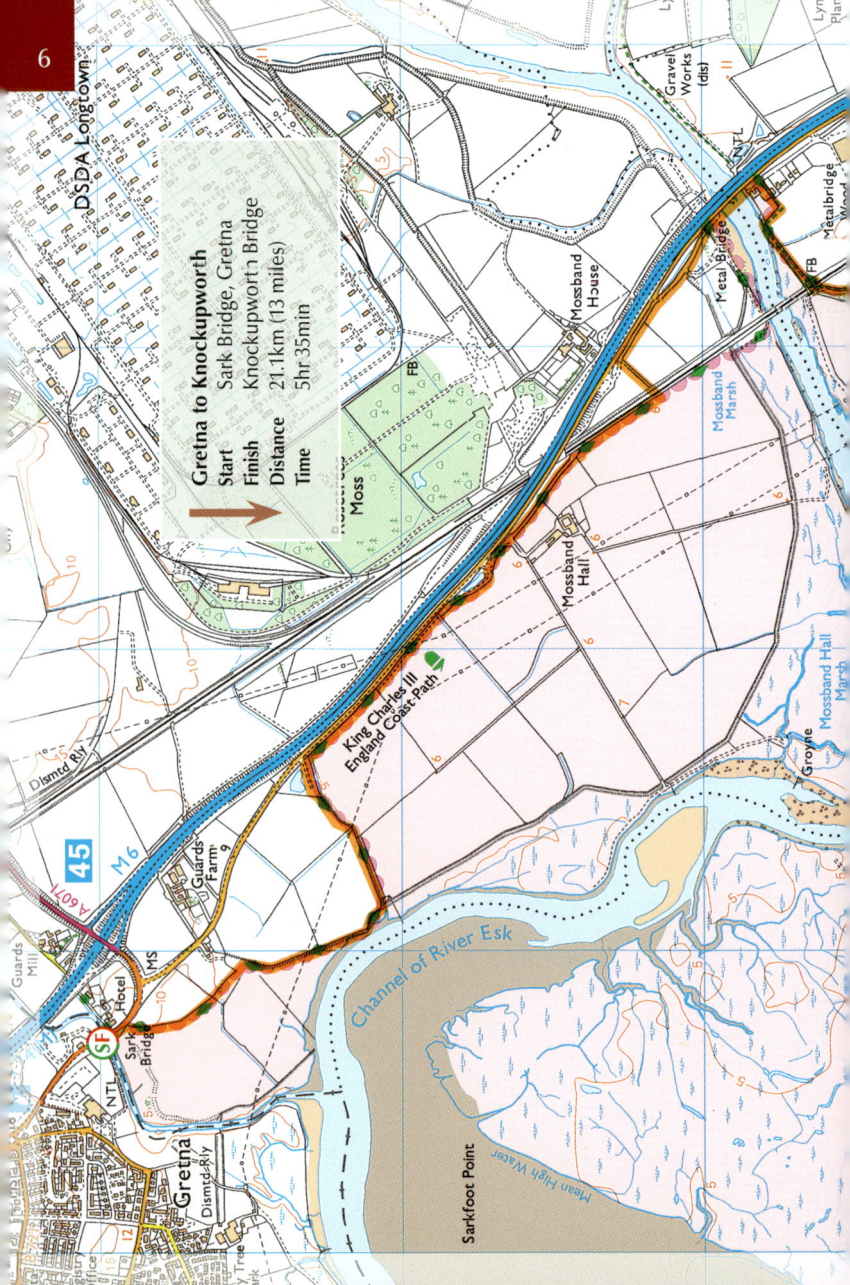

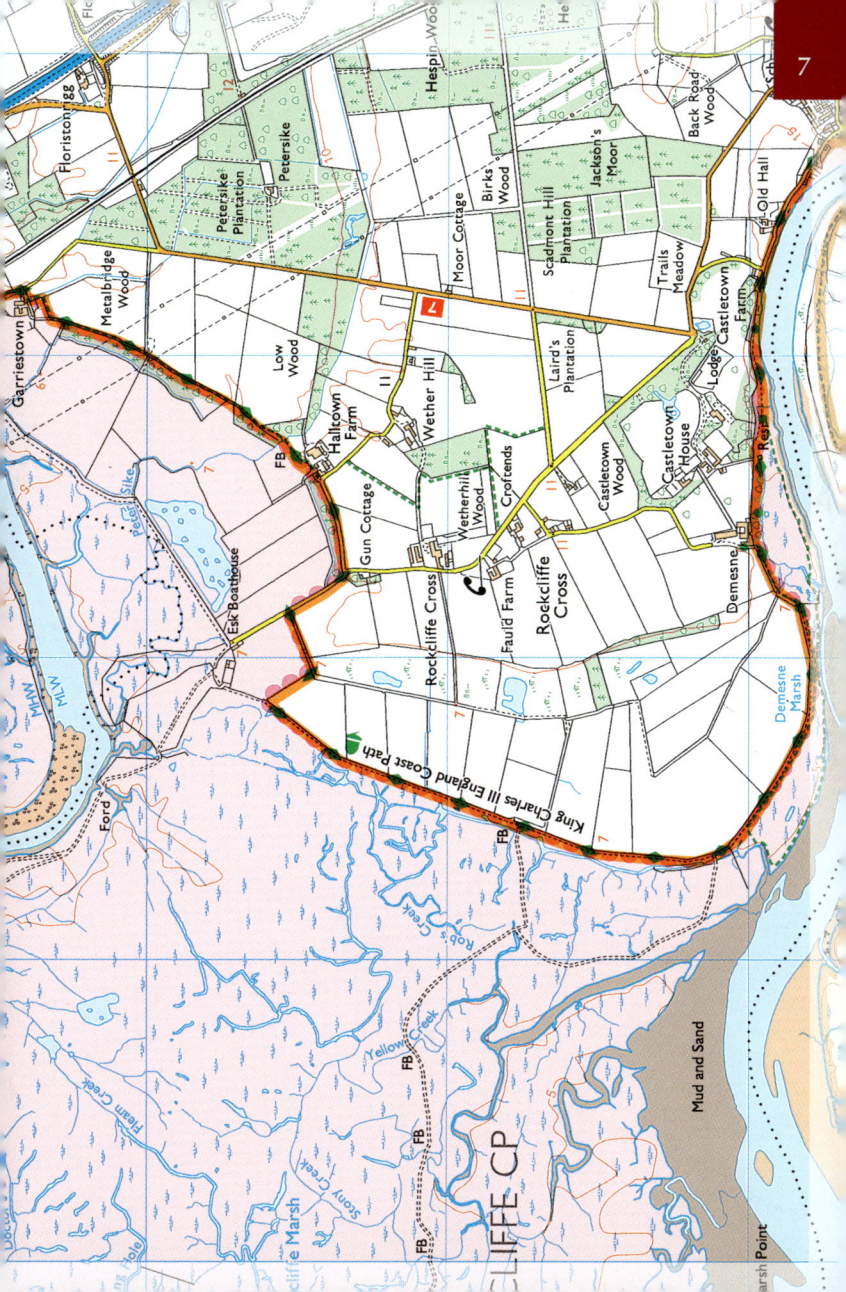

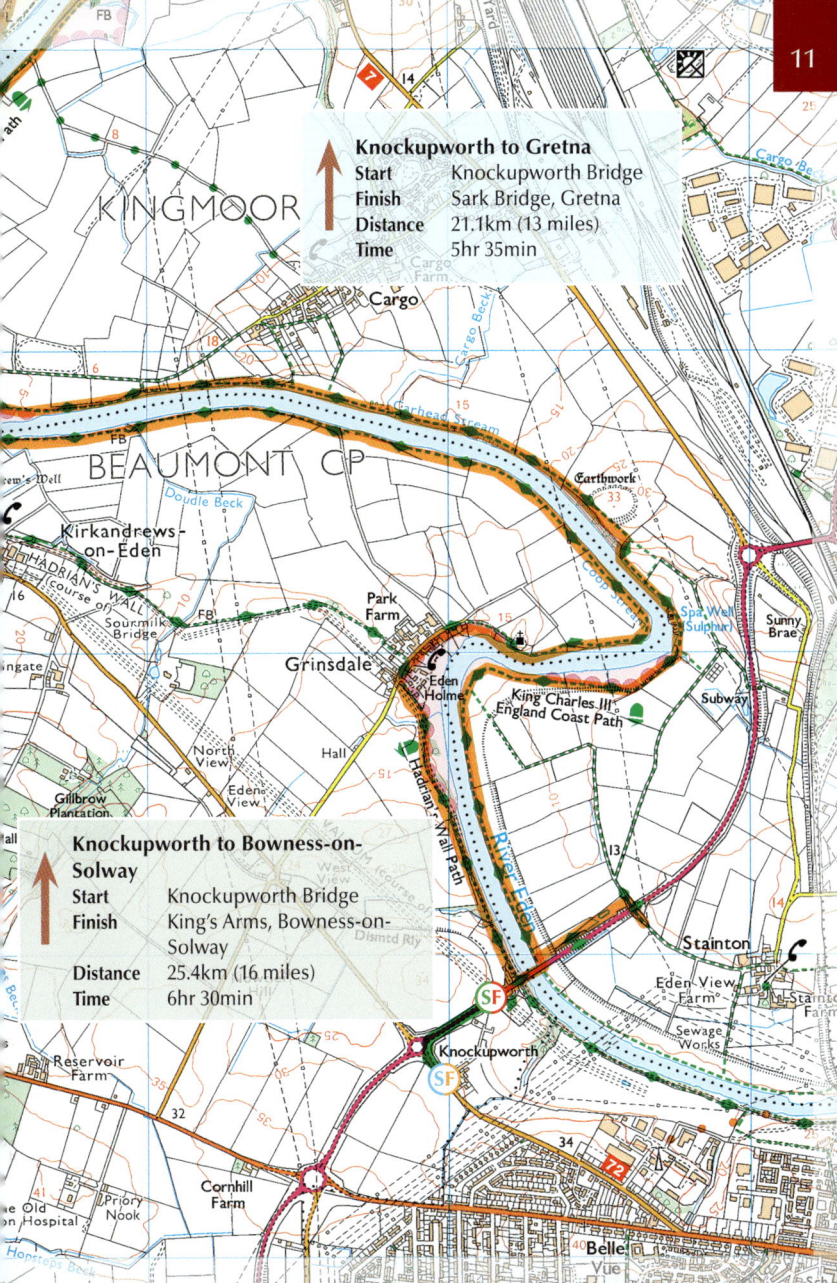

**Bowness-on-Solway to Knockupworth**
Start      King's Arms, Bowness-on-Solway
Finish     Knockupworth Bridge
Distance   25.4km (16 miles)
Time       6hr 30min

High tide route
Use as main route until ECP opens

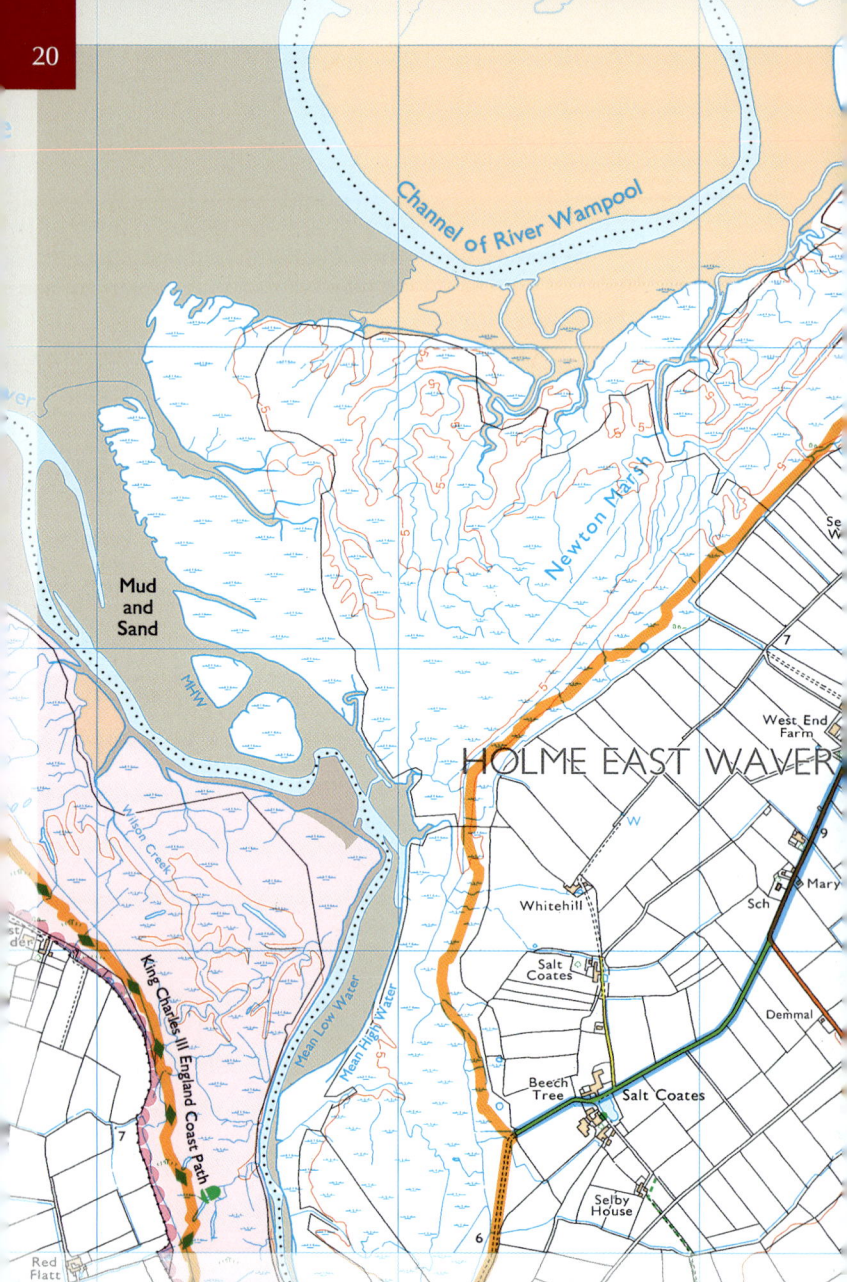

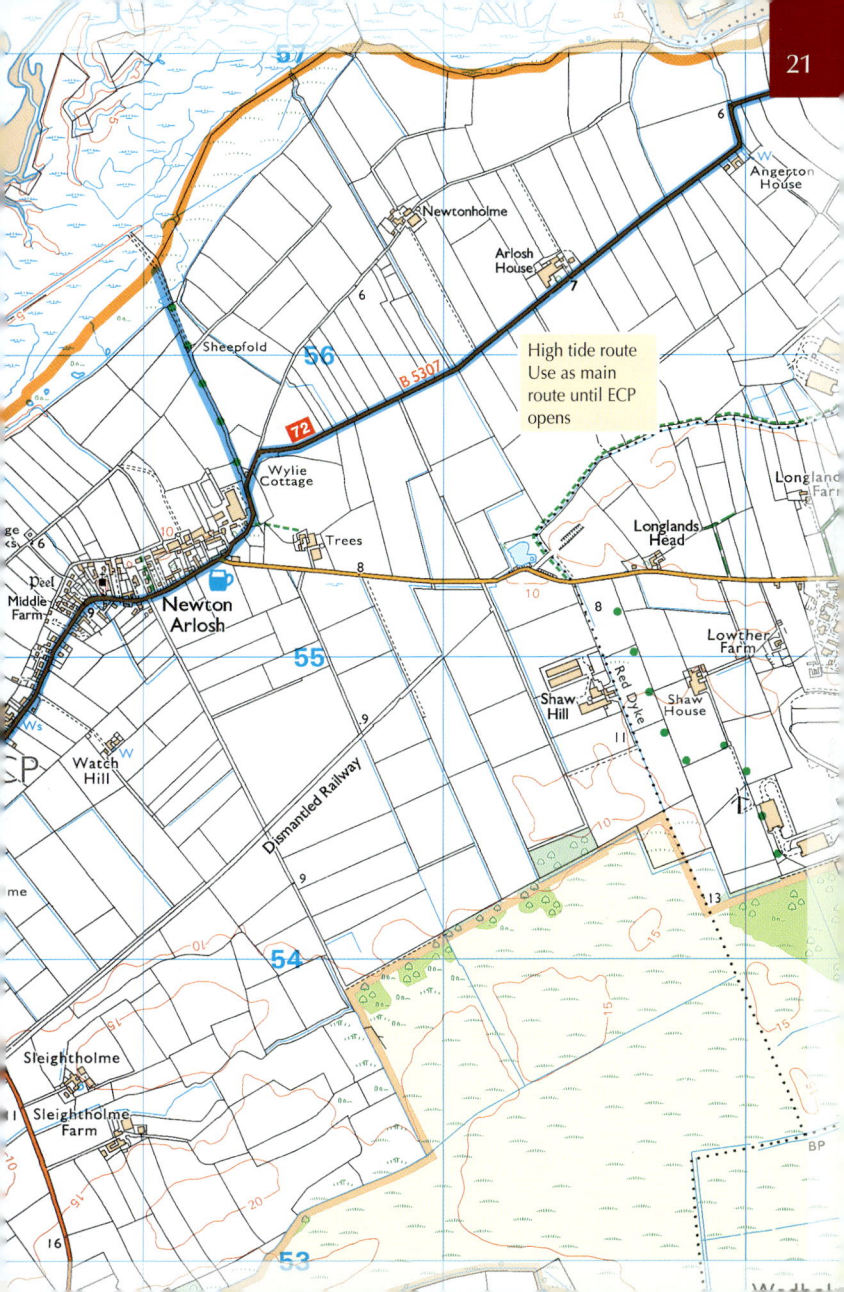

## Abbeytown to Silloth

| | |
|---|---|
| **Start** | Abbeytown riverside |
| **Finish** | Criffel Street/Station Road crossroads, Silloth |
| **Distance** | 16km (10 miles) |
| **Time** | 4hr 30min |

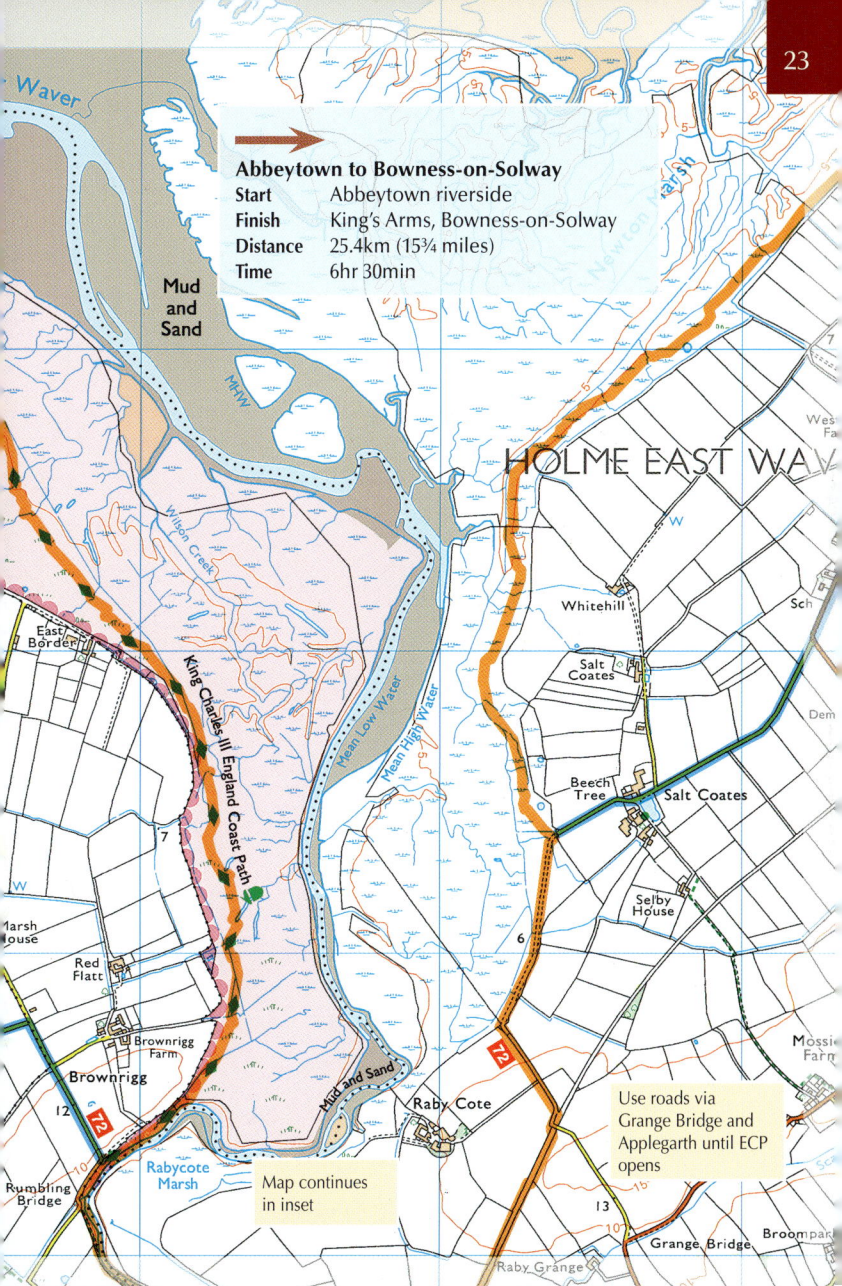

24

Tickhill Scar

Grune Point

Grune Cast

Mean High W.M.

King Charles III England Coast Path

Grune House

Skinburness Creek

Calvo Creek

Lands common to the Parishes of HOLME ABBEY, HOLME LOW and HOLME ST CUTHBERT

FB

Sea Dyke End

Sea Dyke

Great Cotes

FB

Skinburnessbank

Skinburness

East Cote Farm

East Cote

Driving Range

SILLOTH-ON-SOLWAY CP

Groyne

Cote Lighthouse

# 25

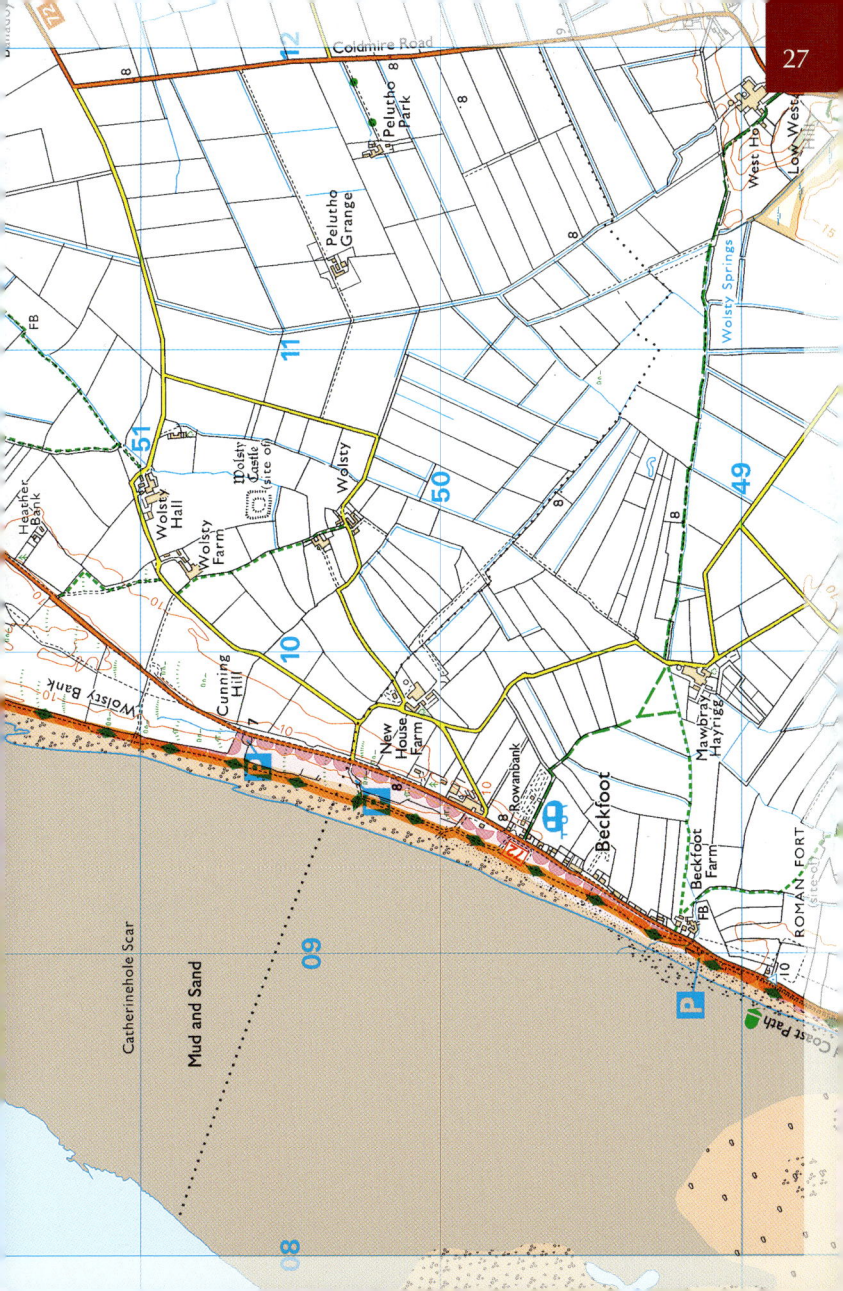

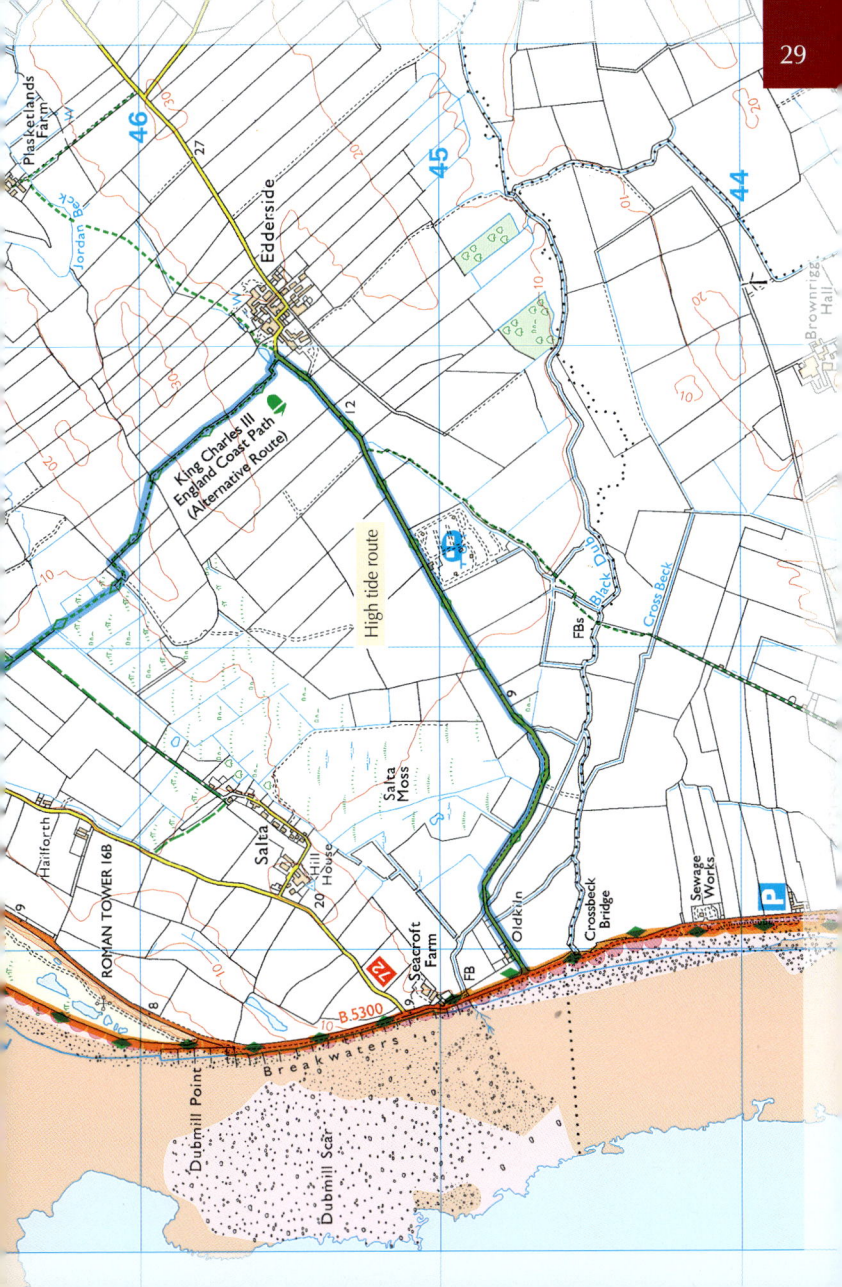

## Maryport to Silloth

**Start** Maryport old harbour bridge
**Finish** Criffel Street/Station Road crossroads, Silloth
**Distance** 20.8km (13 miles)
**Time** 5hr 30min

## Maryport to Whitehaven

**Start** Maryport old harbour bridge
**Finish** Bransty Row, Whitehaven
**Distance** 25.7km (16 miles)
**Time** 6hr 50min

33

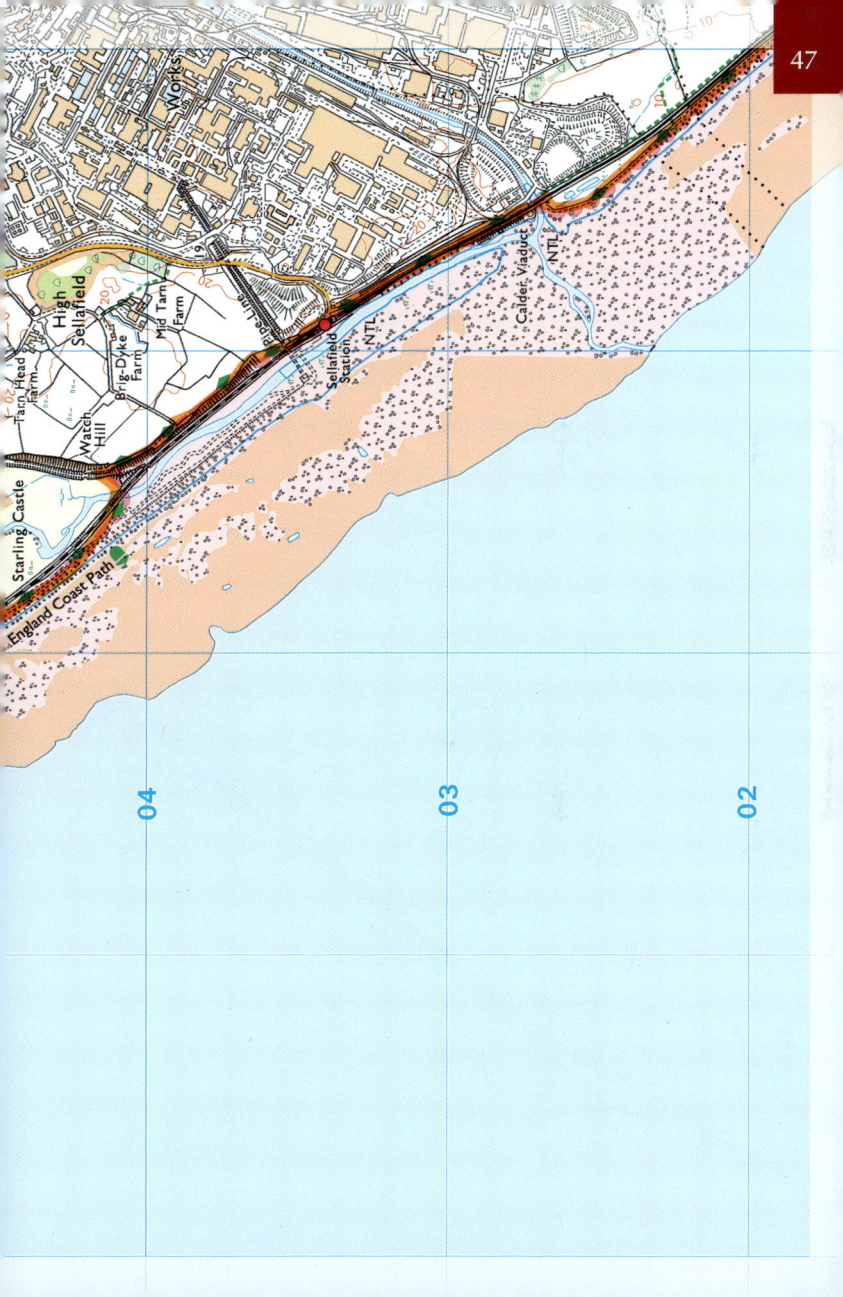

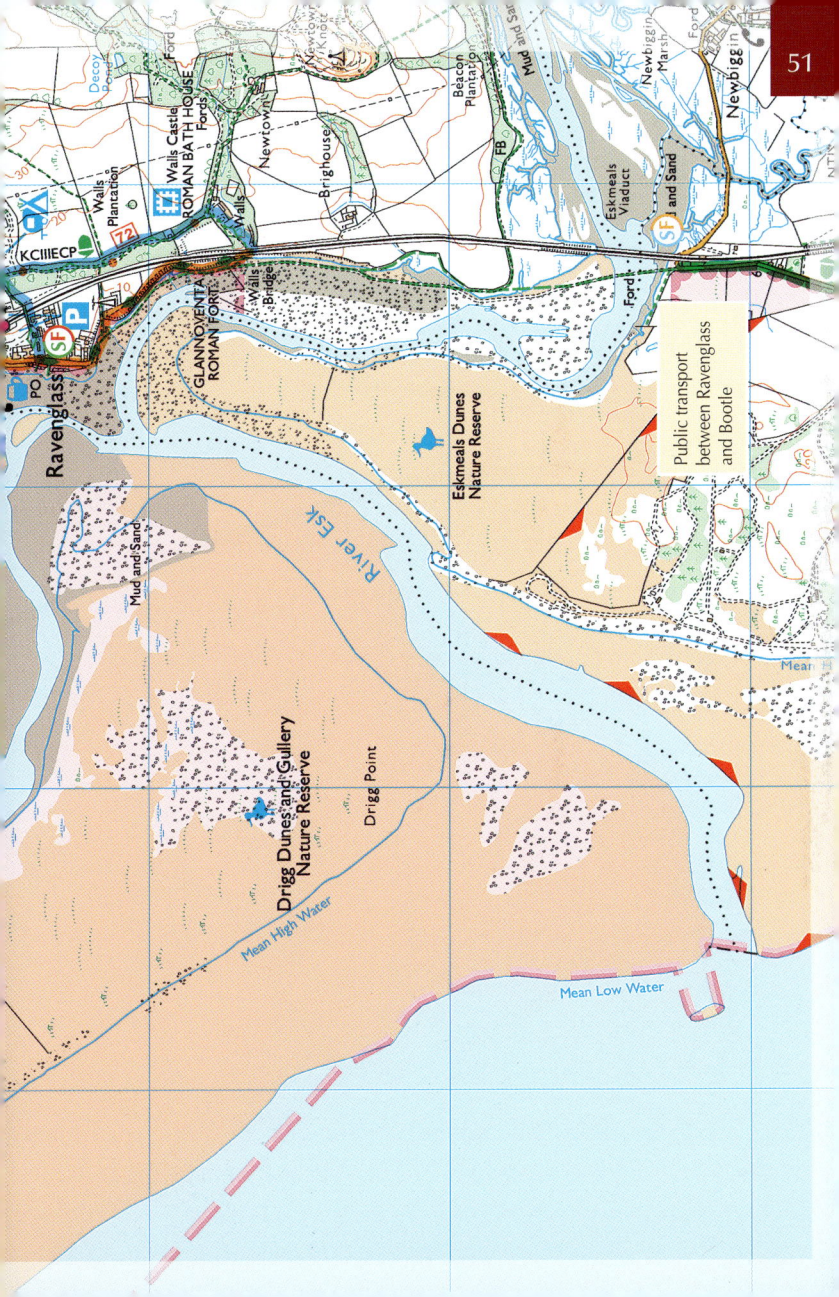

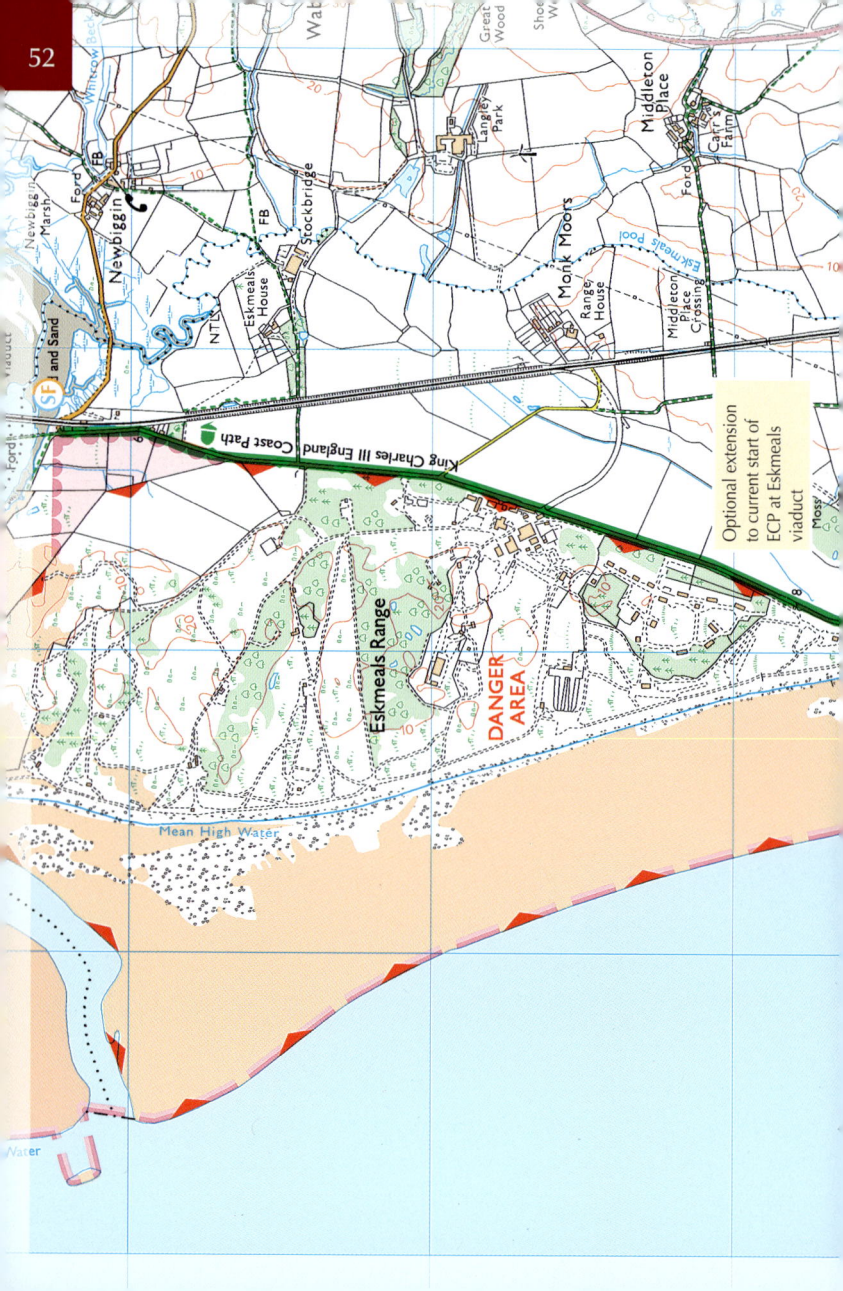

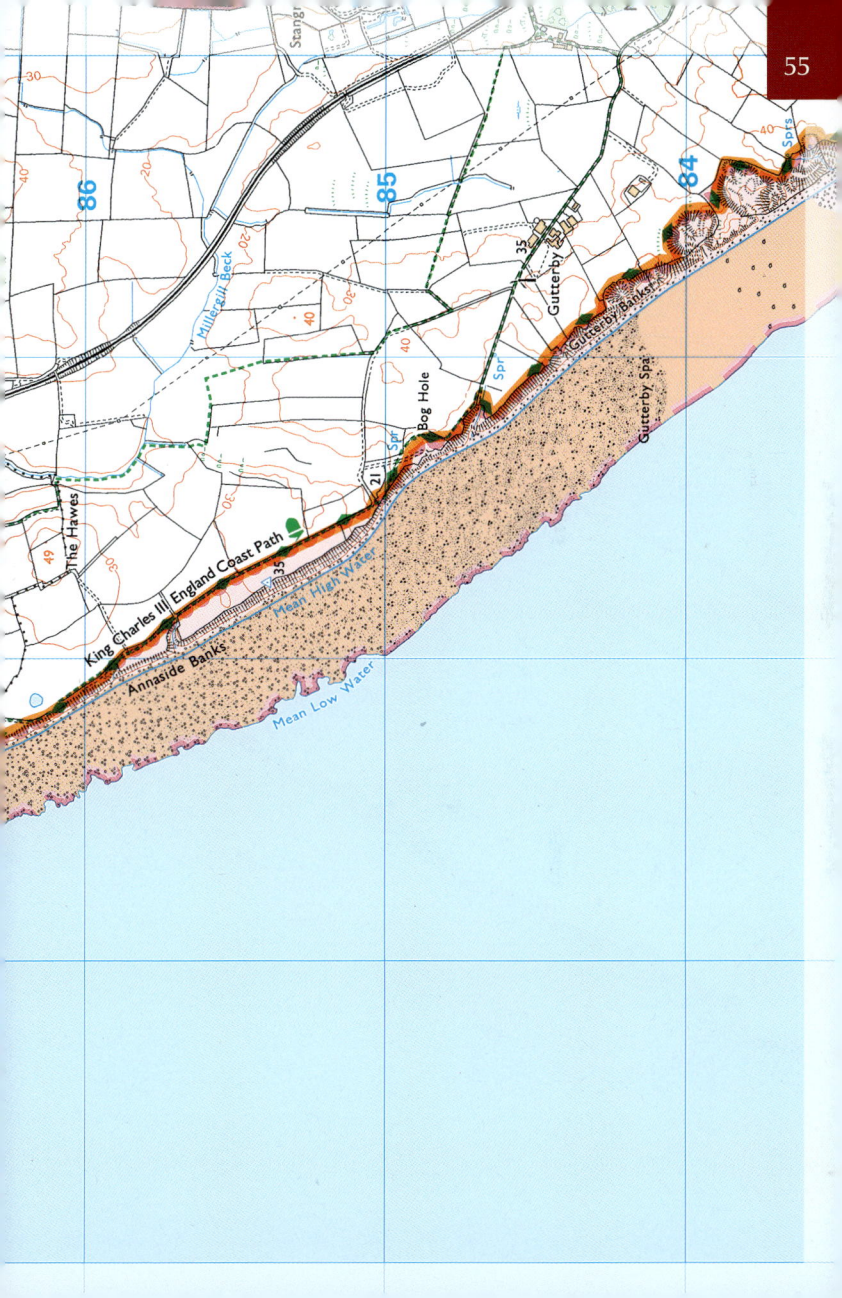

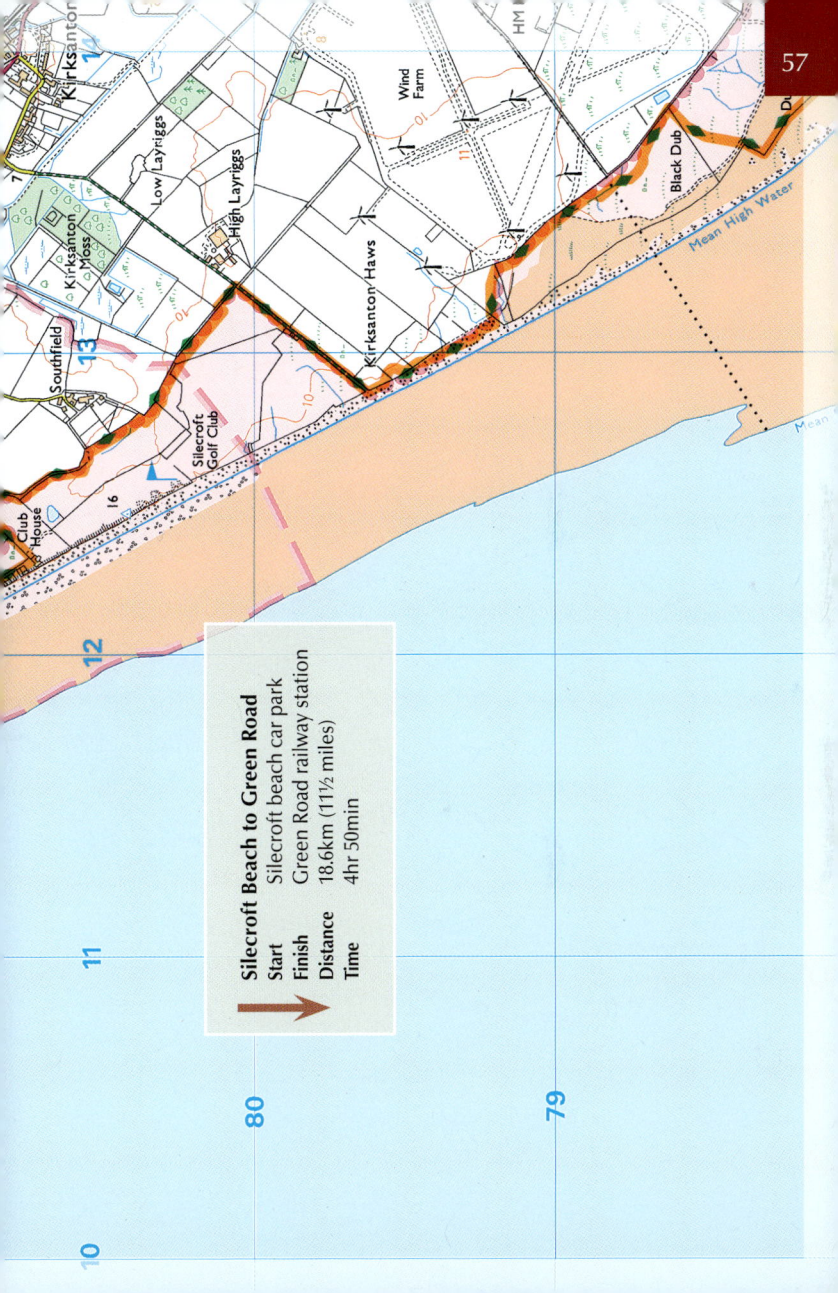

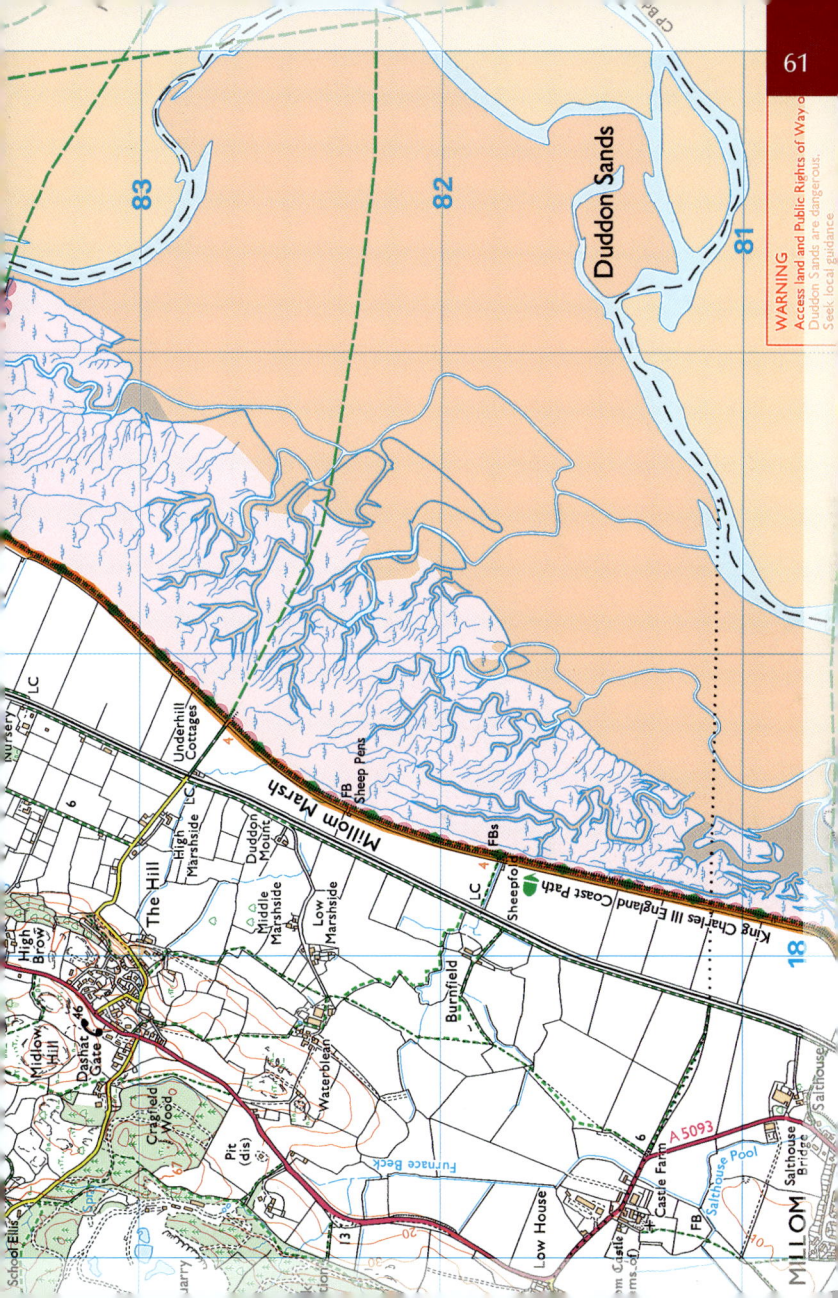

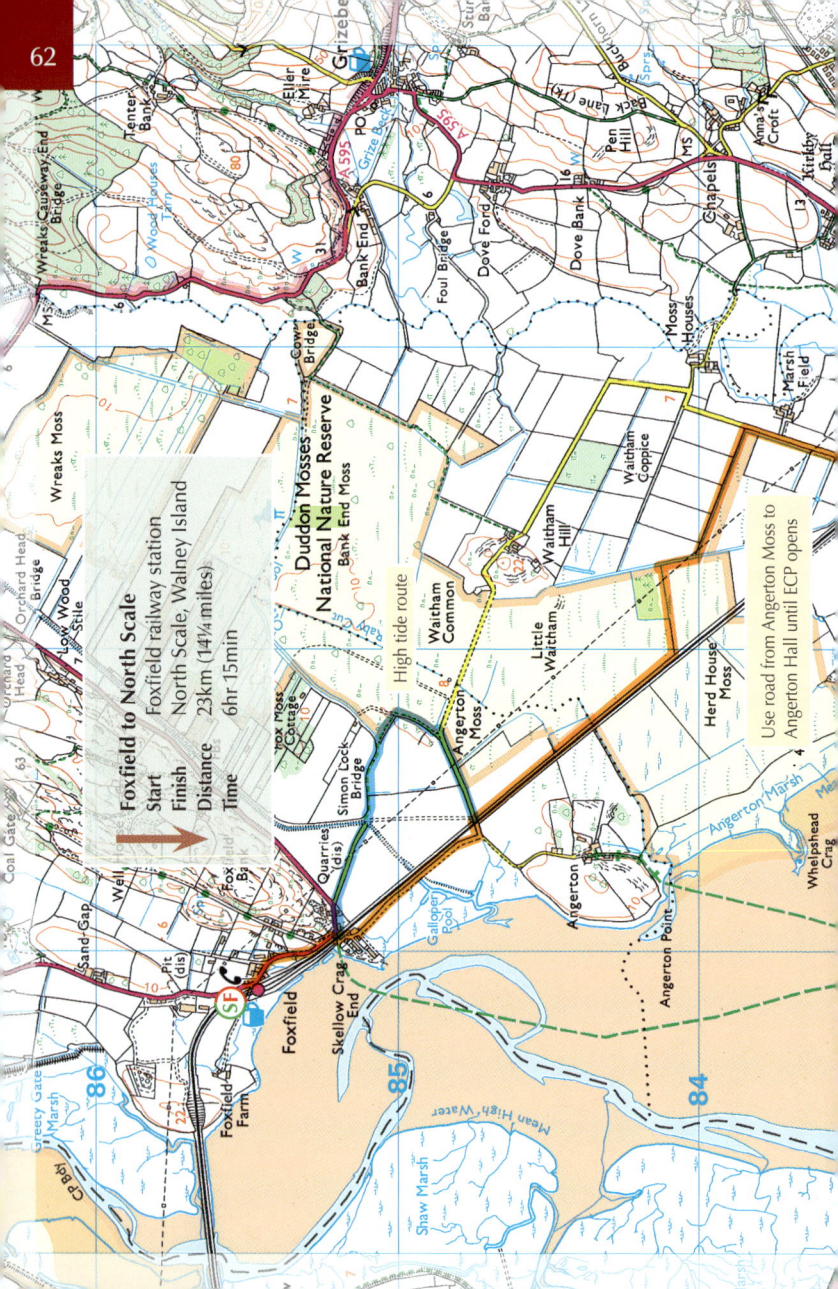

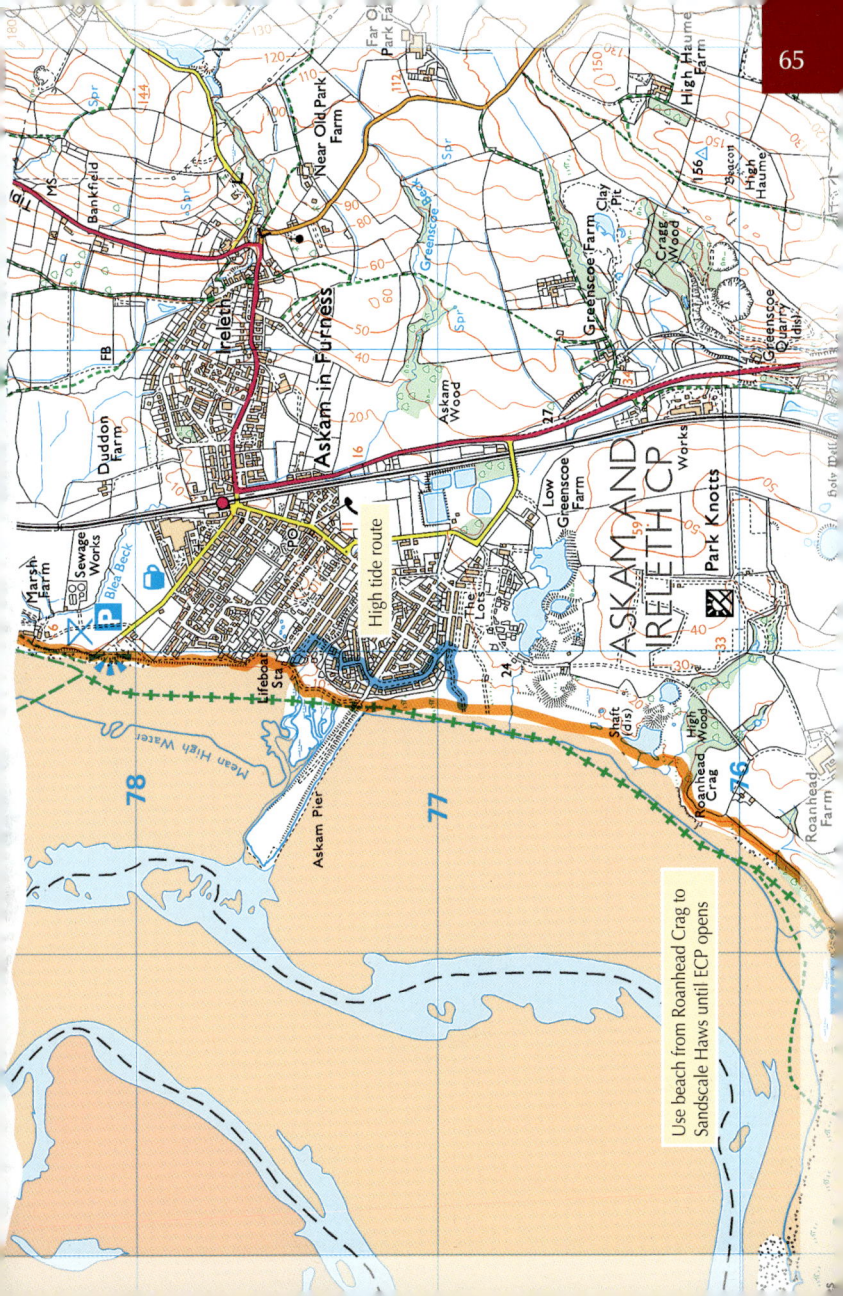

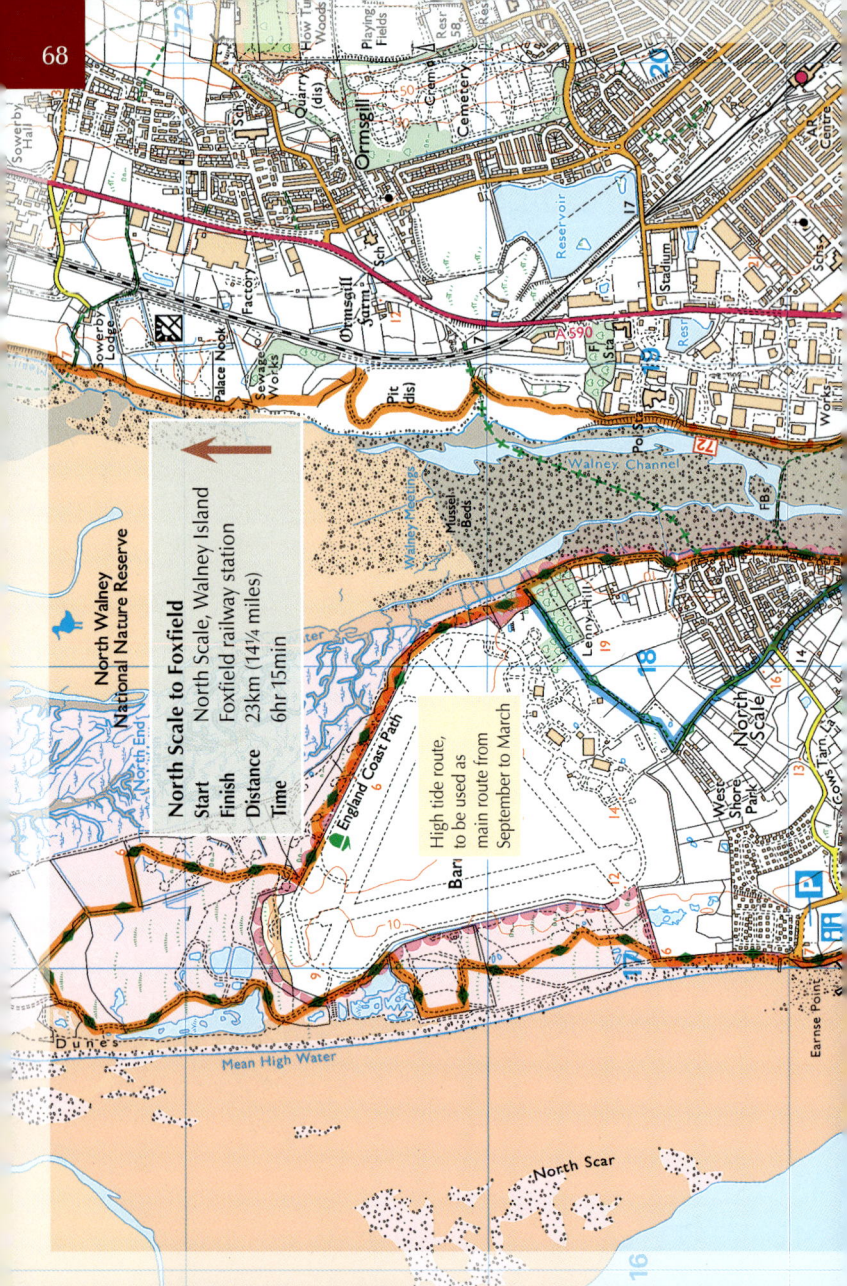

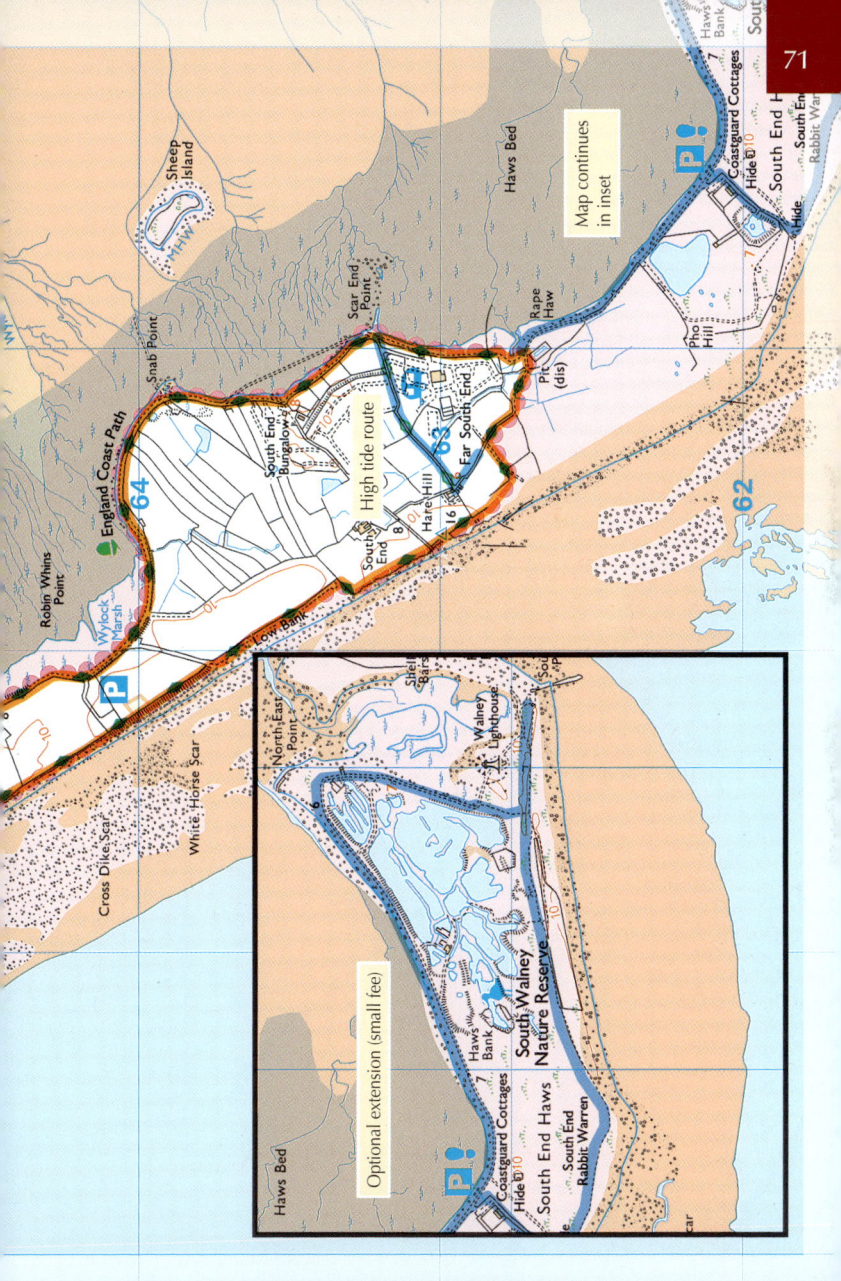

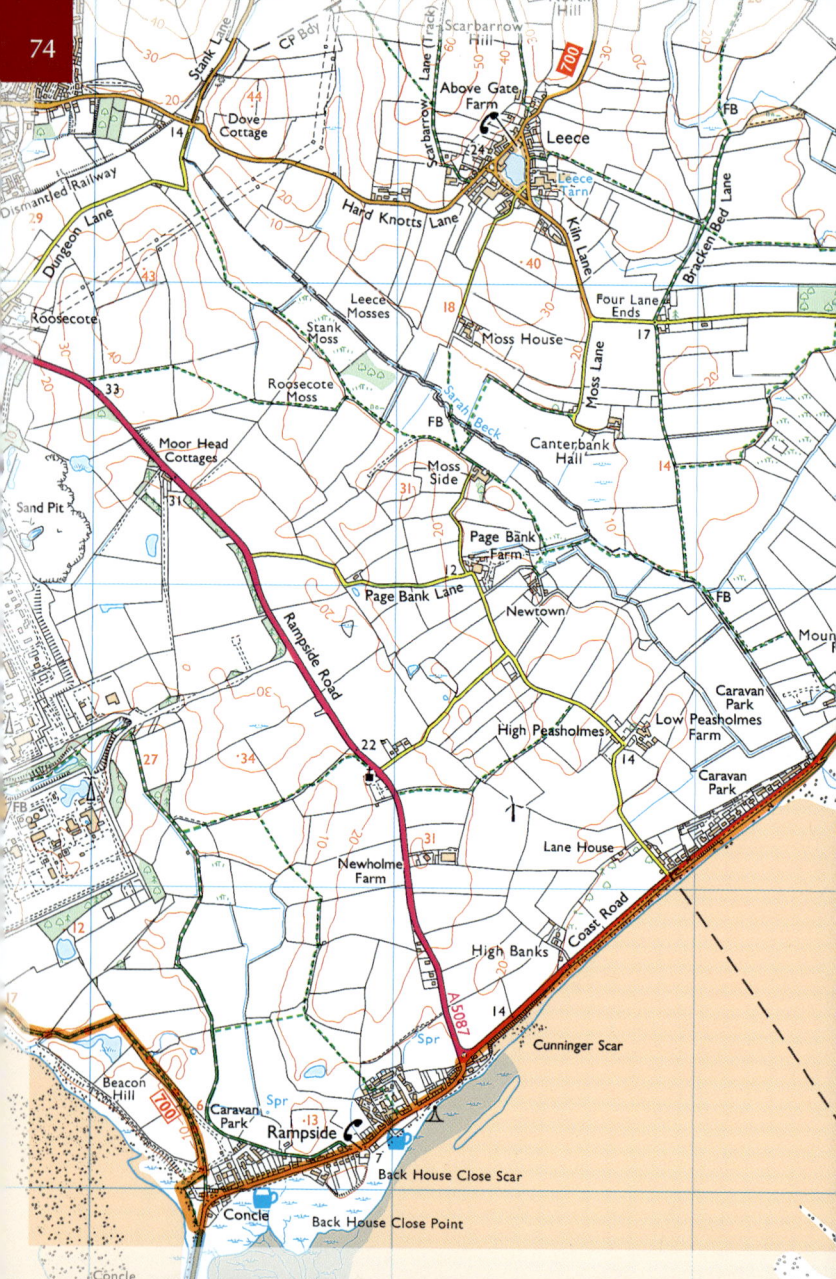

## 75

- Deep Meadow Beck
- art Carrs Beck
- Bracken Hill
- FB
- Sea Mill
- Caravan Park
- Moat Scar
- Seed Hall
- Holiday Park
- Newbiggin
- Sewage Works
- Newbiggin Scar
- Roosebeck House
- FB
- Leonard Scar
- Coast Road
- Goadsbarrow Farm
- Point of Comfort
- Roosebeck
- Point of Comfort Scar
- leasant
- Mean High Water
- Mean Low Water
- Roosebeck Sands
- CP B.dy
- Motte

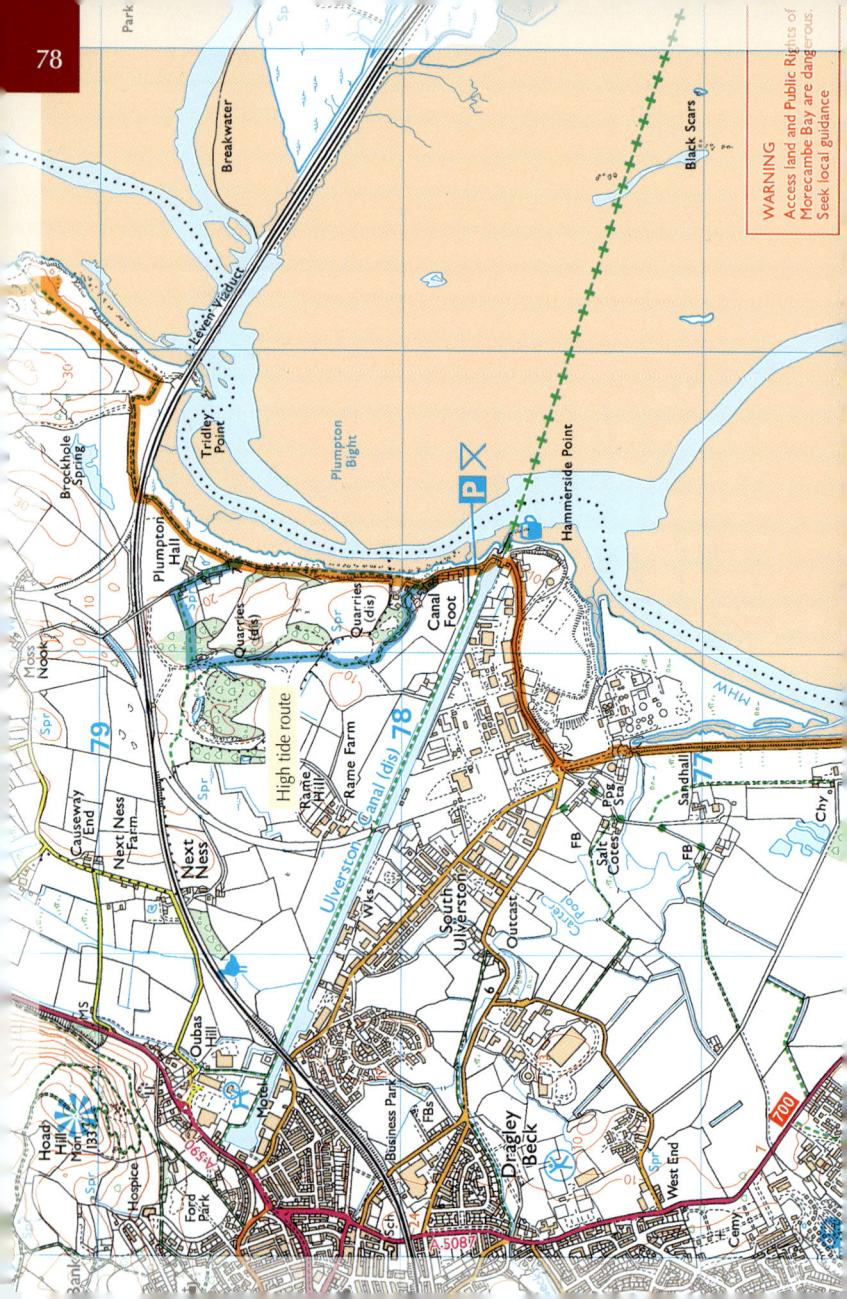

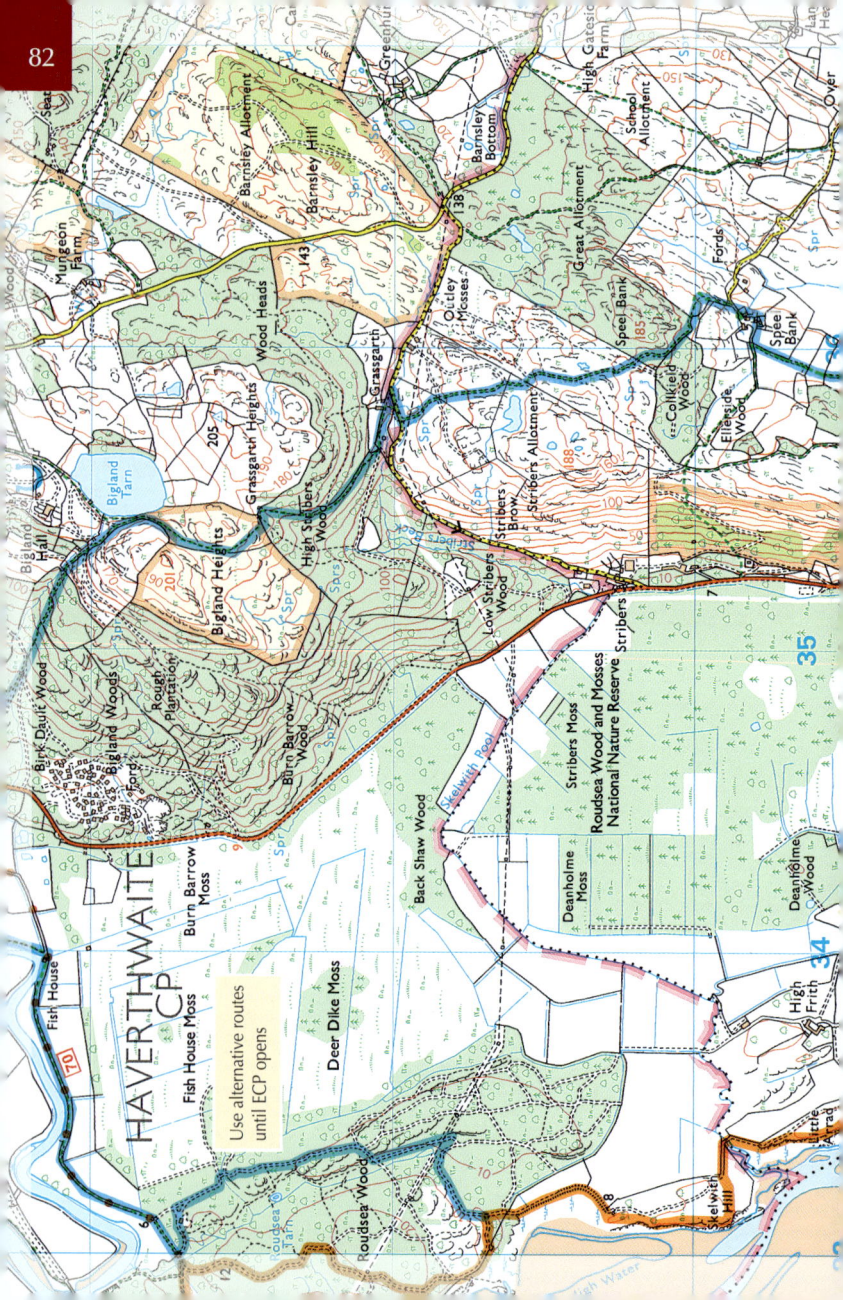

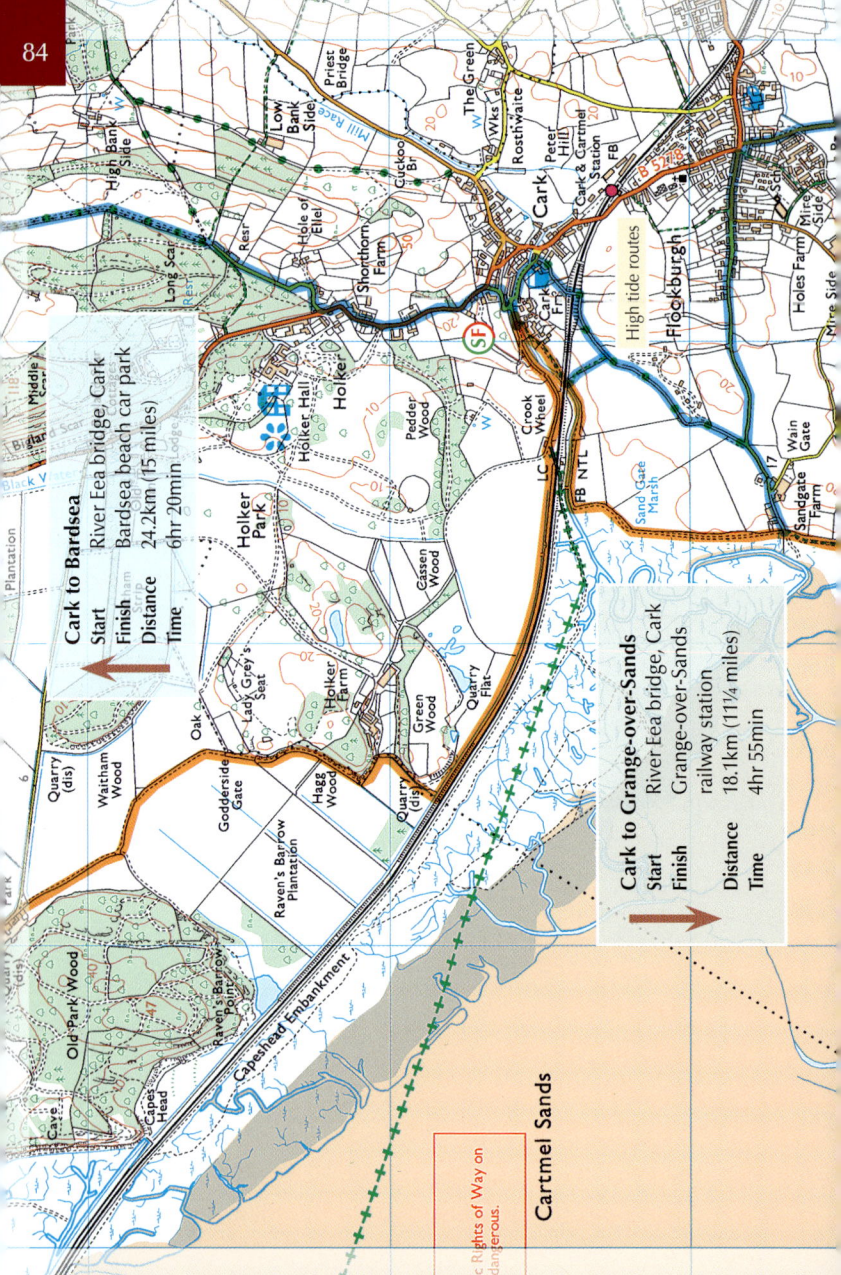

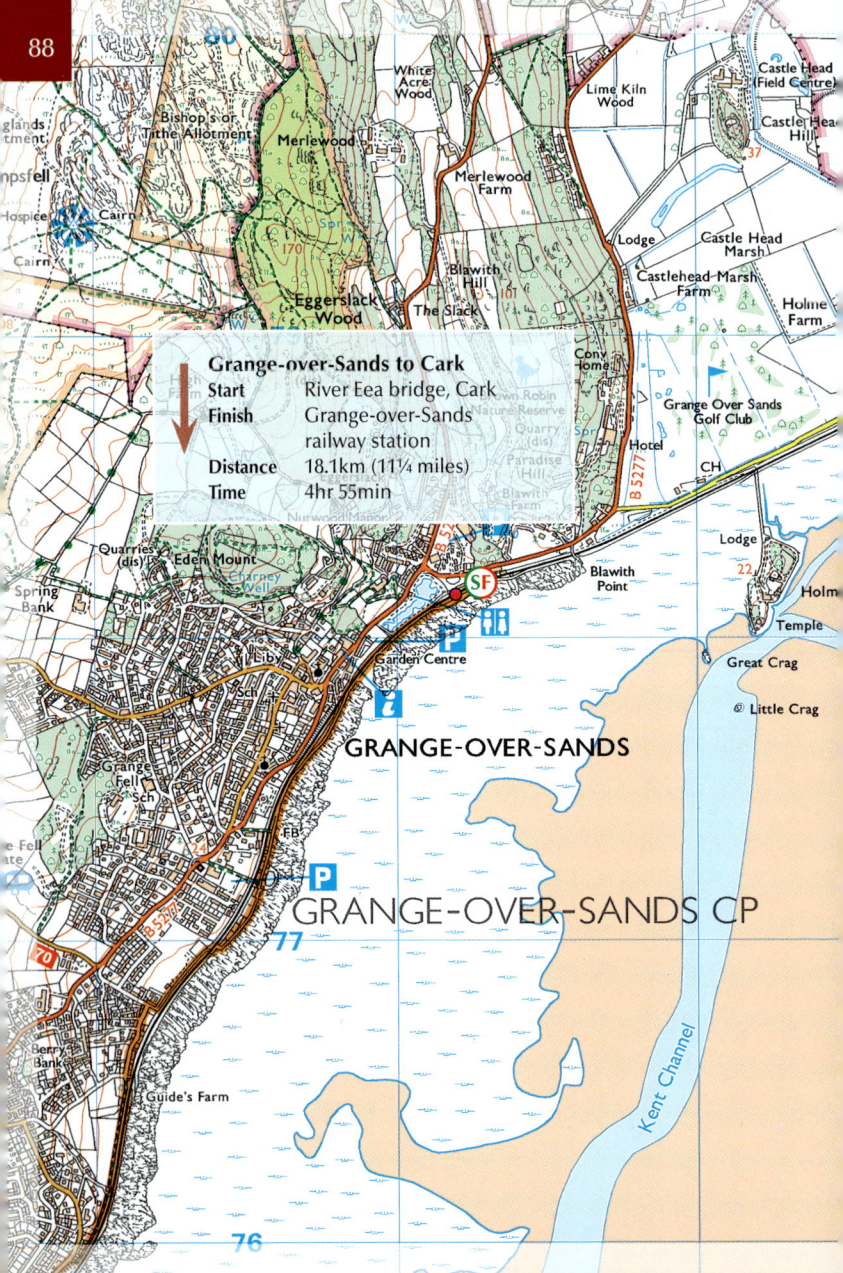

# LEGEND OF SYMBOLS USED ON ORDNANCE SURVEY 1:25,000 (EXPLORER) MAPPING

## ROADS AND PATHS — Not necessarily rights of way

| Symbol | Description |
|---|---|
| M1 or A6(M) | Motorway |
| A 35 | Dual carriageway |
| A30 | Main road |
| B 3074 | Secondary road |
| | Narrow road with passing places |
| | Road under construction |
| | Road generally more than 4 m wide |
| | Road generally less than 4 m wide |
| | Other road, drive or track, fenced and unfenced |
| »  » | Gradient: steeper than 20% (1 in 5); 14% (1 in 7) to 20% (1 in 5) |
| Ferry | Ferry; Ferry P – passenger only |
| | Path |

- S  Service Area (motorway)
- S  Service Area (main road)
- **7**  Junction Number
- **T1**  Toll road junction

## RAILWAYS

- Multiple track / Single track — standard gauge
- Narrow gauge or Light rapid transit system (LRTS) and station
- Road over; road under; level crossing
- Cutting; tunnel; embankment
- Station, open to passengers; siding

## PUBLIC RIGHTS OF WAY

- - - - - - - - -  Footpath
– – – – –  Bridleway
+ + + + +  Byway open to all traffic
+ – + – +  Restricted byway

**The representation on this map of any other road, track or path is no evidence of the existence of a right of way**

## ARCHAEOLOGICAL AND HISTORICAL INFORMATION

| Symbol | Description | Symbol | Description | Symbol | Description |
|---|---|---|---|---|---|
| ✣ | Site of antiquity | VILLA | Roman | ☆ | Visible earthwork |
| ⚔ 1066 | Site of battle (with date) | Castle | Non-Roman | | |

Information provided by English Heritage for England and the Royal Commissions on the Ancient and Historical Monuments for Scotland and Wales

## OTHER PUBLIC ACCESS

• • • Other route with public access (not normally shown in urban areas)
The exact nature of the rights on these routes and the existence of any restrictions may be checked with the local highway authority. Alignments are based on the best information available

♦ ♦ National Trail / (✦) Scotland's Great Trails ♦ ♦ Recreational Route

◇ ◇ Alternative (England Coast Path only)

• • • Traffic-free cycle route

[1] National cycle network route number - traffic free      [1] National cycle network route number - on road

- - - - - - - Permissive footpath   ⎫ Footpaths and bridleways along which
                                    ⎬ landowners have permitted public use
— — — Permissive bridleway          ⎭ but which are not rights of way. The agreement may be withdrawn

### Scotland

In Scotland, everyone has access rights in law* over most land and inland water, provided access is exercised responsibly. **This includes walking, cycling, horse-riding and water access, for recreational and educational purposes, and for crossing land or water.** Access rights do not apply to motorised activities, hunting, shooting or fishing, nor if your dog is not under proper control. The **Scottish Outdoor Access Code** is the reference point for responsible behaviour, and can be obtained at **www.outdooraccess-scotland.com** or by phoning your local Scottish Natural Heritage office.   *Land Reform (Scotland) Act 2003

National Trust for Scotland, always open / limited opening - observe local signs

Forestry Commission Land normally open - / Woodland Trust Land observe local signs

### England, Scotland & Wales

 Firing and test ranges in the area. Danger! Observe warning notices
Champs de tir et d'essai. Danger! Se conformer aux avertissements
Schieß und Erprobungsgelände. Gefahr! Warnschilder beachten
Visit **www.access.mod.uk** for information

## ACCESS LAND

### England & Wales

Access land portrayed on this map is intended as a guide to land normally available for access on foot, for example access land created under the Countryside and Rights of Way Act 2000, and land managed by National Trust, Forestry Commission and Woodland Trust. Some restrictions will apply; some land shown as access land may not have open access rights; always refer to local signage.

Access land      Access information point      Access land in woodland area

Coastal margin

All land within the 'coastal margin' (where it already exists) is associated with the England Coast Path and is by default access land, but in some areas it contains land not subject to access rights – for example cropped land, buildings and their curtilage, gardens and land subject to local restrictions. Furthermore the coastal margin is often steep, unstable and not readily accessible. Please do not assume all the area shaded is accessible and take careful note of conditions and local signage on the ground.

For more information on coastal access check with the local authority or visit:
**http://www.nationaltrail.co.uk/england-coast-path** and **www.openaccess.naturalengland.org.uk**

## ACCESS LAND (continued)

The depiction of rights of access does not imply or express any warranty as to its accuracy or completeness. Observe local signs and follow the Countryside Code.
Visit **www.naturalengland.org.uk/ourwork/enjoying/countrysidecode**

 Access permitted within managed controls, for example, local byelaws
Visit **www.access.mod.uk** for information

## BOUNDARIES

— + — + — National

— · — · — County (England)

— — — — Unitary Authority (UA), Metropolitan District (Met Dist), London Borough (LB) or District
(Scotland & Wales are solely Unitary Authorities)

· · · · · · · · · · Civil Parish (CP) (England) or Community (C) (Wales)

▬▬▬  ▬▬▬ National Park boundary

## VEGETATION

Limits of vegetation are defined by positioning of symbols

- Coniferous trees
- Non-coniferous trees
- Coppice
- Orchard
- Scrub
- Bracken, heath or rough grassland
- Marsh, reeds or saltings

## ARCHAEOLOGICAL AND HISTORICAL INFORMATION

52 ·   Ground survey height
284 ·  Air survey height

Surface heights are to the nearest metre above mean sea level. Where two heights are shown, the first height is to the base of the triangulation pillar and the second (in brackets) to the highest natural point of the hill

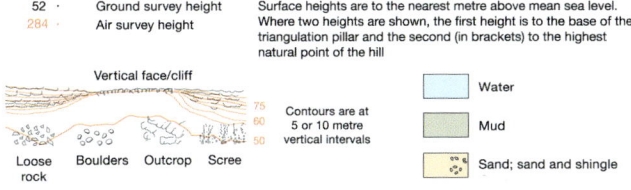

Vertical face/cliff

Loose rock | Boulders | Outcrop | Scree

Contours are at 5 or 10 metre vertical intervals

- Water
- Mud
- Sand; sand and shingle

## SELECTED TOURIST AND LEISURE INFORMATION

- Building of historic interest
- Cadw
- Heritage centre
- Camp site
- Caravan site
- Camping and caravan site
- Castle / fort
- Cathedral / Abbey
- Nature reserve
- National Trust
- Other tourist feature
- Parking
- Park and ride, all year
- Park and ride, seasonal
- Picnic site
- Preserved railway

## SELECTED TOURIST AND LEISURE INFORMATION (continued)

| Symbol | Description | Symbol | Description |
|---|---|---|---|
| | Craft centre | PC | Public Convenience |
| | Country park | | Public house/s |
| | Cycle trail | | Recreation / leisure / sports centre |
| | Mountain bike trail | | Roman site (Hadrian's Wall only) |
| | Cycle hire | | Slipway |
| | English Heritage | | Telephone, emergency |
| | Fishing | | Telephone, public |
| | Forestry Commission Visitor centre | | Telephone, roadside assistance |
| | Garden / arboretum | | Theme / pleasure park |
| | Golf course or links | | Viewpoint |
| | Historic Scotland | V | Visitor centre |
| i | Information centre, all year | | Walks / trails |
| i | Information centre, seasonal | | World Heritage site / area |
| U | Horse riding | | Water activites |
| | Museum | | Boat trips |
| | National Park Visitor Centre (park logo) e.g. Yorkshire Dales | | Boat hire |

(For complete legend and symbols, see any OS Explorer map).

# LISTING OF CICERONE GUIDES

**BRITISH ISLES CHALLENGES, COLLECTIONS AND ACTIVITIES**

Great Walks on the England Coast Path
Map and Compass
The Big Rounds
The Book of the Bivvy
The Book of the Bothy
The Mountains of England and Wales:
  Vol 1 Wales
  Vol 2 England
The National Trails
Walking the End to End Trail
Cycling Land's End to John o' Groats

**SHORT WALKS SERIES**

15 Short Walks Hadrian's Wall
15 Short Walks in the Lake District: Keswick, Borrowdale and Buttermere
15 Short Walks in the Lake District: Windermere Ambleside and Grasmere
15 Short Walks Lake District: Coniston and Langdale
15 Short Walks in Arnside and Silverdale
15 Short Walks in the Ribble Valley
15 Short Walks in Nidderdale
15 Short Walks in Northumberland: Wooler, Rothbury, Alnwick and the coast
15 Short Walks in the Yorkshire Dales: Grassington, Skipton, Malham and Ilkley
15 Short Walks in the Peak District: Bakewell and the White Peak
15 Short Walks on the Malvern Hills
15 Short Walks in Cornwall: Falmouth and the Lizard
15 Short Walks in Cornwall: Land's End and Penzance
15 Short Walks in the South Downs: Brighton, Eastbourne and Arundel
15 Short Walks in the Surrey Hills
15 Short Walks on Dartmoor North: Okehampton and Chagford
15 Short Walks on Dartmoor South: Ivybridge and Princetown
15 Short Walks on Exmoor
15 Short Walks Winchester
15 Short Walks in Bannau Brycheiniog: Brecon Beacons
15 Short Walks in Pembrokeshire: Tenby and the south
15 Short Walks in Dumfries and Galloway
15 Short Walks in the Trossachs: Callander and Aberfoyle
15 Short Walks on the Isle of Mull
15 Short Walks on the Orkney Islands
15 Short Walks on the Shetland Islands

**SCOTLAND**

Ben Nevis and Glen Coe
Cycling in the Hebrides
Cycling the North Coast 500
Great Mountain Days in Scotland
Mountain Biking in Southern and Central Scotland
Mountain Biking in West and North West Scotland
Not the West Highland Way: A Mountain High Way
Scotland
Scotland's Best Small Mountains
Scotland's Mountain Ridges
Scottish Wild Country Backpacking
Skye's Cuillin Ridge Traverse
The Borders Abbeys Way
The Great Glen Way
The Great Glen Way Map Booklet
The Hebridean Way
The Hebrides
The Isle of Mull
The Isle of Skye
The Skye Trail
The Southern Upland Way
The West Highland Way
The West Highland Way Map Booklet
Walking Ben Lawers, Rannoch and Atholl
Walking in the Cairngorms
Walking in the Pentland Hills
Walking in the Scottish Borders
Walking in the Southern Uplands
Walking in Torridon, Fisherfield, Fannichs and An Teallach
Walking Loch Lomond and the Trossachs
Walking on Arran
Walking on Harris and Lewis
Walking on Jura, Islay and Colonsay
Walking on Mull, Coll and Tiree
Walking on Rum and the Small Isles
Walking on the Orkney and Shetland Isles
Walking on Uist and Barra
Walking the Cape Wrath Trail
Walking the Corbetts
  Vol 1 South of the Great Glen
  Vol 2 North of the Great Glen
Walking the Fife Pilgrim Way
Walking the Galloway Hills
Walking the John o' Groats Trail
Walking the Munros
  Vol 1 Southern, Central and Western Highlands
  Vol 2 Northern Highlands and the Cairngorms
Winter Climbs in the Cairngorms
Winter Climbs: Ben Nevis and Glen Coe

**NORTHERN ENGLAND ROUTES**

Cycling the Reivers Route
Cycling the Way of the Roses
Hadrian's Cycleway
Hadrian's Wall Path
Hadrian's Wall Path Map Booklet
The Coast to Coast Cycle Route
The Coast to Coast Map Booklet
The Coast to Coast Walk
Walking the Dales Way
The Dales Way Map Booklet
Walking the Pennine Way
Pennine Way Map Booklet

**LAKE DISTRICT**

Bikepacking in the Lake District
Cycling in the Lake District
Great Mountain Days in the Lake District
Joss Naylor's Lakes, Meres and Waters of the Lake District
Lake District Winter Climbs
Lake District:
  High Level and Fell Walks
  Low Level and Lake Walks
Mountain Biking in the Lake District
Outdoor Adventures with Children — Lake District
Scrambles in the Lake District —
  North
  South
Trail and Fell Running in the Lake District
Walking The Cumbria Way
Walking the Lake District Fells —
  Borrowdale
  Buttermere
  Coniston
  Keswick
  Langdale
  Mardale and the Far East
  Patterdale
  Wasdale
Walking the Tour of the Lake District

## NORTH-WEST ENGLAND AND THE ISLE OF MAN

Cycling the Pennine Bridleway
Isle of Man Coastal Path
The Lancashire Cycleway
The Lune Valley and Howgills
Walking in Cumbria's Eden Valley
Walking in Lancashire
Walking in the Forest of Bowland and Pendle
Walking on the Isle of Man
Walking on the West Pennine Moors
Walking the Ribble Way
Walks in Silverdale and Arnside

## NORTH-EAST ENGLAND, YORKSHIRE DALES AND PENNINES

Cycling in the Yorkshire Dales
Great Mountain Days in the Pennines
Mountain Biking in the Yorkshire Dales
The Cleveland Way and the Yorkshire Wolds Way
The Cleveland Way Map Booklet
The North York Moors
Trail and Fell Running in the Yorkshire Dales
Walking in County Durham
Walking in Northumberland
Walking in the North Pennines
Walking in the Yorkshire Dales:
  North and East
  South and West
Walking St Cuthbert's Way
Walking St Oswald's Way and Northumberland Coast Path

## DERBYSHIRE, PEAK DISTRICT AND MIDLANDS

Cycling in the Peak District
Dark Peak Walks
Scrambles in the Dark Peak
Walking in Derbyshire
Walking in the Peak District -
  White Peak East
  White Peak West

## WALES AND WELSH BORDERS

Cycle Touring in Wales
Cycling Lon Las Cymru
Great Mountain Days in Snowdonia
Hillwalking in Shropshire
Mountain Walking in Snowdonia
Offa's Dyke Path
Offa's Dyke Map Booklet
Scrambles in Snowdonia
Snowdonia: 30 Low-level and Easy Walks — North, South
The Cambrian Way
The Pembrokeshire Coast Path
The Pembrokeshire Coast Path Map Booklet
The Snowdonia Way
The Wye Valley Walk
Walking Glyndwr's Way
Walking in Carmarthenshire
Walking in Pembrokeshire
Walking in the Brecon Beacons
Walking in the Wye Valley
Walking on Gower
Walking the Severn Way
Walking the Shropshire Way
Walking the Wales Coast Path

## SOUTHERN ENGLAND

20 Classic Sportive Rides
  in South East England
  in South West England
Cycling in the Cotswolds
Mountain Biking on the North Downs
Mountain Biking on the South Downs
The North Downs Way
The North Downs Way Map Booklet
The South Downs Way
The South Downs Way Map Booklet
The Cotswold Way
The Cotswold Way Map Booklet
The Ridgeway National Trail
The Ridgeway Map Booklet
The Thames Path
The Thames Path Map Booklet
The Two Moors Way
Two Moors Way Map Booklet
Walking the South West Coast Path
South West Coast Path Map Booklet
  Vol 1: Minehead to St Ives
  Vol 2: St Ives to Plymouth
  Vol 2: St Ives to Plymouth
  Vol 3: Plymouth to Poole
Suffolk Coast and Heath Walks
The Kennet and Avon Canal
The Lea Valley Walk
The Peddars Way and Norfolk Coast Path
The Pilgrims' Way
Walking Hampshire's Test Way
Walking in Essex
Walking in Kent
Walking in London
Walking in Norfolk
Walking in the Chilterns
Walking in the Cotswolds
Walking in the Isles of Scilly
Walking in the New Forest
Walking in the North Wessex Downs
Walking on Dartmoor
Walking on Guernsey
Walking on Jersey
Walking on the Isle of Wight
Walking the Dartmoor Way
Walking the Jurassic Coast
Walking the Sarsen Way
Walks in the South Downs National Park
Walking on La Palma
Walking on Lanzarote and Fuerteventura
Walking on Tenerife
Walking on the Costa Blanca
Walking the Camino dos Faros
Portugal's Rota Vicentina
The Camino Portugues
Walking in Portugal
Walking in the Algarve
Walking on Madeira
Walking on the Azores

## SWITZERLAND

Switzerland's Jura Crest Trail
The Swiss Alps
Tour of the Jungfrau Region
Trekking the Swiss Via Alpina
Walking in Arolla and Zinal
Walking in the Bernese Oberland — Jungfrau region
Walking in the Engadine — Switzerland
Walking in Ticino
Walking in Zermatt and Saas-Fee

## TECHNIQUES

Fastpacking
The Mountain Hut Book

## MINI GUIDES

Alpine Flowers
Navigation

## MOUNTAIN LITERATURE

A Walk in the Clouds
Abode of the Gods
Fifty Years of Adventure
The Pennine Way — the Path, the People, the Journey
Unjustifiable Risk?

For full information on all our guides, books and eBooks, visit our website:
**www.cicerone.co.uk**

## WALKING THE KING CHARLES III ENGLAND COAST PATH: NORTH WEST

This map booklet accompanies Ange Harker's guidebook to walking the King Charles III England Coast Path, from Gretna to Chester. The guidebook features 1:50,000 OS mapping alongside detailed step-by-step route description and lots of planning and other information about local culture, wildlife and the protected coastline.

*Humphrey Head is one of Morecambe Bay's most dramatic limestone outcrops, seen here from below on its western side (Stage 15)*

# CICERONE

Trust Cicerone to guide your next adventure, wherever it may be around the world...

Discover guides for hiking, mountain walking, backpacking, trekking, trail running, cycling and mountain biking, ski touring, climbing and scrambling in Britain, Europe and worldwide.

**Connect with Cicerone online and find inspiration.**

- buy books and ebooks
- articles, advice and trip reports
- GPX files and updates
- regular newsletter

**cicerone.co.uk**